YOUR KNOWLEDGE HAS VALUE

The importance of Virtual Reality in "Ready Player One" by Ernest Cline and its Movie Adaptation

Nicole Piontek

Bibliographic information published by the German National Library:

The German National Library lists this publication in the National Bibliography; detailed bibliographic data are available on the Internet at http://dnb.dnb.de.

ISBN: 9783346578433
This book is also available as an ebook.

© GRIN Publishing GmbH
Nymphenburger Straße 86
80636 München

Print and binding: Books on Demand GmbH, Norderstedt, Germany
Printed on acid-free paper from responsible sources.

The present work has been carefully prepared. Nevertheless, authors and publishers do not incur liability for the correctness of information, notes, links and advice as well as any printing errors.

GRIN web shop: https://www.grin.com/document/1168353

Rheinische Friedrich-Wilhelms-Universität Bonn

Institut für Anglistik, Amerikanistik und Keltologie

The importance of Virtual Reality in Ernest Cline's *Ready Player One*
and its movie adaptation.

Term paper for

Anglophone Media and Popular Cultures

Summer Term 2021

Nicole Piontek

Bonn, 26th August 2021

Table of Contents

1.   Introduction 1

2.   Exploration of Virtual Reality...2

3.   Virtual Reality in *Ready Player One* 4

   3.1.   The OASIS..4

   3.2.   Work and Education 6

   3.3.   Friends and Family...8

   3.4.   Video Games 11

   3.5.   Escapism 13

4.   Conclusion 16

Bibliography..18

1. Introduction

This paper aims at pointing out the difference of the importance of the OASIS in Ernest Cline's Ready Player One and its movie adaptation. In both versions of the story the OASIS plays a prominent role. Nevertheless, the novel offers a more profound representation of the virtual world which results in a different portrayal of the novel's characters and their relationship with others and the world as a whole. In how far does the representation of the virtual world and its technological attributes differ? Where does the movie make cuts and what focus does each version choose?

Firstly, a theoretical approach on Virtual Reality will offer a better understanding of the background technology in Ready Player One. Furthermore, it enables a comparison to our present reality. What is actually possible in our world? Are the technological portrayals in the novel and the movie realistic from our point of view, or is it purely hypothetical? Are there aspects our society could even learn from?

In the main part of this paper, I will investigate different aspects of the OASIS. The first chapter is going to describe how the OASIS works in both versions and how it is used by the people.

Afterwards, this paper will focus on social aspects. For this, the second chapter explores the representation of working possibilities as well as educational possibilities in and around the OASIS. Especially when it comes to the school system the novel offers a very detailed description, whereas the movie seems to lack this notion. In how far can the movie compensate this, and what effects does it have on the novel? The next chapter focuses on the meaning of friends and family within the virtual reality. The protagonist of the story interacts mainly with two other characters which he both got to know in the OASIS. Thus, the OASIS must establish a platform and the technological possibilities to create such a deep friendship. What is it exactly that makes communication and interaction possible in the OASIS? Furthermore, the chapter will analyse how both versions portrayed the first meeting in the real world. There ought to be differences in the effect of the meeting, as the characters meet earlier in movie than in the novel.

There are two more interesting themes in Ready Player One. One is undoubtedly video games. The whole story is based upon this notion and the idea reappears on almost every page. How do video games coexist and correlate with the virtual reality? Do they only influence the hunt or the character's relationships as well? The second theme is the motif of Escapism. In the novel Wade repeatedly mentions how he wants to run away from earth and live entirely in the

OASIS. In addition, reality is described being in catastrophic shape. Around such a scenario the OASIS seems like a safe haven.

2. Exploration of Virtual Reality

Virtual Reality is a complex technological topic. The basic ideas and concepts of it are demonstrated in the following chapter. In broader context virtual reality is a simulation of reality that is computer generated (cf. Langer 20). An important factor of VR is immersion. Users are set into a media environment both psychological and physical (cf. ibid. 21). Moreover, users are fully inside this new reality that all their awareness is concentrated inside the virtual reality (cf. ibid. 23). Furthermore, VR is also seen as a field that expands "human experience beyond the limits that physical matter imposes on human nature." (Crawford 29) Thus, virtual reality can mirror or enhance our reality. Subsequently, Dörner defines the technology as follows: "Virtual Reality refers to immersive, interactive, multi-sensory, viewer-centered, three-dimensional computer generated environments and the combination of technologies required to build these environments." (Dörner 13) Hence, to use virtual reality one needs high technology.

Broken down into general equipment, without going into specific technical details, one needs computer hardware and software, sensors and displays for the usage of virtual reality (cf. Langer 21). To put it even simpler: "Virtual reality is the 'goggle and gloves' technology that attempts to capture every sensation possible." (Fairfield 69). The technology is being developed since the 1990s and especially in this century innovations are coming on a yearly basis. Still, Fairfield argues that the development of VR is only slowly progressing because "the current digital revolution is social, not technological." (ibid. 69f.) According to him, the most important aspect of an VR experience is that it is shared: "Shared experiences, not completely immersive experiences, are driving the current push into the most successful mobile apps." (ibid. 70) Therefore, Fairfield appeals to put the focus in research on the development of such shared experiences. In an earlier essay when VR was not yet accessible for most of the people Stevens writes:

> Then groups of people could together explore the wonders of a cell, the inside of volcanoes, and the depths of the ocean with virtual reality. Such a group activity would provide the extra stimulation of experiencing a place with others-more like going on a vacation or a field trip than using a computer. (Stevens 439)

Here, one can see that the wish for shared virtual experiences existed already in the beginning of the development. While talking about VR and society, the term virtual world is often used as another expression for virtual reality.

A virtual world is similar to a virtual reality, but its focus lies in social environments. It is generally regarded as an alternative to reality (cf. Chaturvedi 673). Chaturvedi defines this alternative as follows: "[…] their ability to offer an alternative means to communicate, collaborate, and even to organize economic activity." (ibid. 673f.). Thus, virtual worlds offer a place "[…] in which individuals, groups, and even organizations interact in virtual nonphysical spaces." (Saunders 1079) Summing up, the main difference of virtual reality and virtual worlds is that virtual worlds have "more social and fewer immersive features than pure virtual reality." (Fairfield 71) This kind of virtual environments focus on social interaction and shared experiences. Moreover, according to Downey we are now in the third-generation virtual worlds (cf. Downey 59), which means that it became mainstream, and the technology experiences an "explosion of user growth" (ibid.). Alongside more investments are coming and more money can be used for its development. At present, virtual worlds are used for gaming, education and society matters (cf. ibid. 61). However, virtual reality is used in various areas as well.

Today, virtual reality can be found in different fields. I.e., the technology is used to "allow people working in safety-critical industries" (Nasyrov 353), in the sense that they can train virtually in these dangerous environments before facing the difficult circumstances in reality. VR also comes along with new possibilities and chances "for human creativity and global social interaction in science, business, and government." (Saunders 69) Although the technology has this great set of options, it is mostly used for entertainment and tends to neglect its possibilities (cf. Nasyrov 353). For instance, Saunders sees great possibilities for the usage of VR in schools and education in general. He appeals to political forces to strengthen research and development in this area (cf. Saunders 69). He also states that to successfully instate VR in education there is also the need of changing the overall curriculum (cf. ibid. 71). Thus, the technology itself cannot change a society on its own no matter how far advanced it may be. It needs the adaptation of society as well. However, virtual reality is not the only growing technology which correlates with our reality.

There are more versions that describe the connection of reality and technical innovations, such as Mixed Reality, Augmented Reality and Extended Reality. Fairfield sums theses up with the term "Reality+" (Fairfield 74). According to him our reality has always been influenced by other people, tools, or technical devices. Technology is constantly in further development and our reality is constantly changing and expanding (cf. ibid.).

3. Virtual Reality in *Ready Player One*

3.1.   The OASIS

A large part of the story of *Ready Player One* takes place in virtual reality. This chapter defines this virtual world and points out its concepts. The OASIS, or "The Ontologically Anthropocentric Sensory Immersive Simulation" (Cline 48), is the virtual reality in and around which the story of *Ready Player One* takes place. In both the novel and the movie, the OASIS contains countless different planets and is described thoroughly. In the novel these planets are either generated by the creators of the simulation or ported to the OASIS from already existing sources like World of Warcraft and Everquest (cf. ibid. 49). Furthermore, the author describes the structure of the OASIS repeatedly on different occasions very detailed (i.e., ibid. 49 and 57). The movie introduces the virtual reality as follows: "It's a place where the limits of reality are your own imagination." (Spielberg 00:03:42). Overall, size, and technical possibilities are similarly described, and the broad and general technical devices and possibilities are existing in our present reality as well, although not as advanced as described here (cf. Fink). The movie furthermore visualizes the OASIS with bright colours which create a magical atmosphere. This atmosphere is even more strengthened by heroic music (cf. Spielberg 00:03:42). Thus, the OASIS is considered a wonderful place with limitless possibilities in both the novel and the movie. However, the technology was originally intended to serve another function.

The storytelling stresses the notion of the OASIS being originally an online game, or to be more precise a MMORPG (Massively Multiplayer Online Role-Playing Game), which evolved into a second reality (cf. Cline 1) where people do almost everything "except for eating, sleeping, and bathroom breaks" (Spielberg 00:04:56). Thus, further development of the OASIS led to a device for social interaction rather than an online game. This mirrors Fairfield's argument that society is leading the technology to a direction of social aspects: "Consumers have clearly indicated that they seek socially rich experiences." (Fairfield 70) Moreover, the novel mentions the OASIS alongside human's basic needs: "work, food, electricity, and reliable OASIS access" (Cline 21) and states that the younger generations do not even know a life without the virtual reality (cf. ibid. 34). But not only do young people use the technology. All generations spend a lot of their time in virtual reality. For instance, Mrs. Gilmore, Wade's elderly neighbour, is spending her time in virtual churches (cf. ibid. 23). In addition, the movie portrays people of different age and social background using the OASIS (cf. Spielberg 00:06:26 f.). Therefore, the importance of virtual reality for this society is highlighted from beginning on.

4

One of the most important aspects of the Oasis is identity and anonymity: "Anonymity was one of the major perks of the OASIS." (Cline 28) Users of the virtual reality rarely use their real names or outer appearances. People decide on their own whether they want to share their identity. Still, "real name, fingerprints, and retinal patterns" (ibid. 28) are stored in your account. Thus, the information does exist somewhere in the virtual reality, only hidden and encrypted (cf. ibid. 28). Users chose their identity by creating an avatar in both novel and movie. Thus, Lasko-Harvill argues that people are wearing a kind of costume they can hide behind: "Virtual participants, then, are actors, and their appearance, costume. In view of the multiplicity of possible identities, switching between aspects can be like changing costumes." (Lasko-Harvill 225f.) This costume gives them freedom of choosing not only outer appearance but also personality, as actors can theoretically be whoever they want to be. In the movie this thought is expressed when Aech is talking about Art3mis: "She could actually be a 300-pound dude who lives in his mama's basement in suburban Detroit." (Spielberg 00:41:53) He says that although Art3mis is a pretty young woman in the OASIS does not mean that she has to be the same in reality. Overall, anonymity and the freedom to choose who you want to be, are main reasons for the popularity of virtual realities in general (cf. Patra 1663). Another reason could be the escape from poverty.

The OASIS is portrayed as being accessible for everyone anytime. On closer inspection, not at all: in the novel, people can access the planet Incipio for free, but other than that people must pay transportation fares to access more of the virtual reality (cf. Cline 31). Furthermore, there are also other aspects which can only be accessed with money, such as items and a well-equipped chatroom like Aech's chatroom (cf. ibid. 37). The movie also introduces coins and value in the OASIS, and states: "Artifacts. Those were key. Halliday made sure the OASIS was littered with enough randomly powerful stuff that anyone could win if they had the skills." (Spielberg 00:06:09 - 00:06:19). Following it is described how to obtain coins which is purely by playing the game well, and not limited to transportation fares. Still, people can invest money and lose all of it when dying in the game. This is exemplified with Rick, Wade's aunt's boyfriend, who puts all their savings in the game and loses (cf. Stark 164). Furthermore, there are items and artifacts on auction to buy. Therefore, being rich does still have advantages and there is a difference of being poor and rich in the OASIS just as there is in the real world. Furthermore, the OASIS and the reality share another similarity in financial matters.

The OASIS has its own currency which concurs with the one in the real world. This notion is primarily mentioned in the novel. Furthermore, it not only introduces the currency itself, but states that it is regarded the most secure and stable one (cf. Cline 28). The new currency is put in direct comparison to the one in reality. The author does this by writing that one can possess items which have "just as much value as things in the real world (sometimes more) [...]." (ibid. 27) Here, it is implied that the OASIS can be more valuable than the real world. Patra argues that the replacement of values and currencies is a normal happening when a virtual reality concurs the real world (cf. Patra 1663). Thus, as the OASIS plays a prominent role in people's life, its currency and value are also ought to gain importance. Overall, the novel and the movie portray the basic concept of the OASIS similarly. Both are described as being limitless and of utter importance to all people.

3.2.   Work and Education

After illustrating the basic concept of the OASIS in the previous chapter, working possibilities and educational programmes in the virtual reality will be described here. The novel offers numerous examples of working possibilities in and around the OASIS, whereas the movie only shows how to gain coins with in-game battles. In the following some of the examples of the novel are described: The protagonist's mother used to work for the OASIS: "She had two full-time OASIS jobs, one as a telemarketer, the other as an escort in an online brothel." (Cline 15) Meanwhile, Wade himself had a virtual babysitter (cf. ibid.). Later, he tried to find a part-time job but was unsuccessful finding one. Still, he mentions that there are jobs as "tech support and programming jobs" (ibid. 51). When he clears the first gate, he becomes famous and receives numerous offers for advertisement campaigns, where his face would be used to advertise products (cf. ibid. 131). Furthermore, his friend Aech makes money by "competing in televised PvP arena games after school and on the weekends." (cf. ibid. 37f) Therefore, there are various working possibilities for all ages in and around to the OASIS. People can either perform "virtual labor" (Stark 163) inside the simulation or work in jobs as technical support, repairing, or other jobs related to the OASIS. Still, the movie does not portray these possibilities, just like it is missing the topic of education.

In the novel the OASIS offers possibilities for education in all stages of growing up. Wade states that he was basically raised by the OASIS. Not only did he have a virtual babysitter, but he was also educated with interactive games and had access to "the world's biggest public library." (Cline 15) The overall educational concept for children is all free and accessible for everyone: "[...] the OASIS's interactive educational programs, which any kid could access for free." (ibid.) Saunders predicts a similar education in his article. According to him such a virtual system could bring education to all people in all nations rich and poor (cf. Saunders 69). His vision can be seen in the novel as the school in the OASIS is free for everyone and everyone

6

can have access to all information from home in a secure place. Still, education has a limit in the OASIS, as college is expensive and cannot be attended by all people like school (cf. Cline 29). Thus, the society makes a difference between the education of children and grown-ups. Nevertheless, the OASIS in the novel offers a wide range of possibilities for education for children. Its high school system is even described in more detail.

The importance of education in the virtual reality is strengthened by the detailed description of the school concept. There is a whole planet dedicated to the school, the planet Ludus. Not only is the school overall free for every child, including the covering of transportation costs to the planet (cf. ibid. 31), but it also follows strict rules to ensure safe and secure education. For instance, the school has rules for the outer appearance of avatars. There does exist a dress code, which states that avatars must be human like and correspond to the real gender and age (cf. Cline 28). Furthermore, students must use their real name in school (cf. ibid. 29) and when registering for school they are obligated to share personal information such as real name, address, and Social Security number. This is stored and only the principle has access to the data (cf. ibid.). In addition, the whole planet is a no-PvP zone. Therefore, there is no combat happening on the planet as weapons have no power (cf. ibid. 30). To create the atmosphere of an ordinary high school, the place is designed to look like one. For example, Wade has his own locker, where he keeps textbooks and which he decorates (cf. ibid. 26) like students in typical American high schools do. Although the rules are strict on Ludus, students are allowed to use other parts of the OASIS, such as chatrooms, in school but only while waiting for classes to start. They are reminded with pop up messages when a lesson is about to start: "A message flashed on my display, informing me that the three-minute-warning bell had just rung in my classroom." (ibid. 45) Overall, the planet and the school system are designed to be a safe place for students and the author constructed it thoughtfully. Moreover, Cline also describes the ways of teaching.

The novel illustrates the possibilities of virtual teaching. Teachers are offered anonymity: "Of course, we didn't know who Mr. Avenovich really was or where he lived. We didn't know his real name, or even if "he" was really a man." (ibid. 47) Here, the protagonist tells us, that teachers are not bound to the rules previously described. They can change their identity and use it to disguise themselves. Furthermore, teachers are more motivated as well:

> Unlike their real-world counterparts, most of the OASIS public school teachers seemed to genuinely enjoy their job, probably because they didn't have to spend half their time acting as babysitters and disciplinarians. [...] All the teachers had to do was teach. (Cline 47)

Thus, teachers can totally focus on their teaching and disregard all pedagogical influences. Moreover, there are not only human teachers, but also teachers that are generated by the simulation. Students are not able to detect whether a teacher is real or not. Such a way of teaching has advantages, as Johnson's example shows: He writes about "[…] a lesson in particle physics delivered by Einstein" (Johnson 164). He continues stating that a lesson taught by an avatar that looks like Einstein "could be enormously compelling" (ibid.) and motivating. Moreover, the novel describes field trips, which can be made any day as the simulation allows the students to do so without leaving school grounds (cf. Cline 47f). This teaching tool offers multiple possibilities to give students a more hands on experience (cf. ibid. 48). Johnson supports this opinion and states that virtual reality and immersive learning as a whole can strengthen the learning effect as well as motivation in both students and teachers (cf. Johnson 164). Just as Cline mentions field trips within the OASIS, Johnson writes about lessons within different virtual worlds to support his argument (cf. ibid.). Summing up, the description of the school system in the novel highlights the importance of education and the possibilities VR brings along. In addition, Ludus has yet another function in the novel.

The importance of Ludus is further strengthened in the novel. Cline lets the planet be a central part in the hunt, as the first key is hidden on this planet. On the one hand this strengthens the meaning of Ludus and directs the readers' focus on the school planet, on the other hand it also hints at the main target group of Halliday's hunt. The planet is accessible for everyone; therefore, everyone can get the first key. Still, as on Ludus are only schools, children have an advantage as they spent every day on the planet. However, the movie misses the whole notion of education and its importance. Here, one can find Ludus only very briefly. It can be seen in the scene in which Wade explains the OASIS (cf. Spielberg 00:04:29). One can see the planet for a second which is accompanied by the ringing of a school bell. Other than that, Ludus is not mentioned in the movie. Thus, the novel offers a deeper example of education in virtual reality.

3.3. Friends and Family

By now the previous chapters have shown that life in the OASIS is of utter importance to Cline's and Spielberg's societies. This chapter will further explore the aspect of friends and family in the virtual reality. When it comes to family, the protagonist does not have a real family, neither in the real world nor in virtual reality. In both versions of the story Wade's parents have died and he lives with his aunt in a trailer in the stacks. His aunt does not appear in the OASIS alongside Parzival. Nevertheless, the novel briefly mentions that Wade used to interact with his mother in the OASIS (cf. Cline 18). Still, this is the only mentioning of family withing the simulation.

In contrast, friendship is influenced by virtual reality and technology makes it easy to communicate and interact with each other. The movie introduces this as follows: "[…] this is where we meet each other. It's where we make friends." (Spielberg 00:05:03), and Cline writes in his novel:

> Before long, billions of people around the world were working and playing in the OASIS every day. Some of them met, fell in love, and got married without ever setting foot on the same continent. (Cline 60)

Both quotes show that the OASIS is the place to get to know people. Moreover, one can meet people from all over the world and make even more friends than in the real world. In addition, the technology behind the OASIS makes communication as easy and close to real world interaction as possible. Not only can users write and talk to each other, but they can also make use of gestures and facial expressions. For instance, Aech and Parzival interact as naturally as in real life with one another, as the simulation allows users to speak and communicate nonverbally. This is shown for example when Aech and Parzival high five each other when meeting in Aech's chatroom (cf. ibid. 38). In addition, the communication between Parzival and Art3mis also shows these possibilities as they are grinning at each other (cf. ibid. 96). The movie establishes the same picture of the virtual world. Here, one can see how the avatars move and look like. Everything is fluent and feels like reality while watching it. At 00:16:07 the movie shows that avatars can also touch and interact with each other. Here, Parzival holds Art3mis preventing her to get caught by King Kong (Spielberg 00:16:07). Thus, communication is as easy in the OASIS as it is in the real world in both versions of the story. Furthermore, the notion of friendship can be further analysed by looking at Parzival's friends individually.

The character Aech demonstrates the significance of the virtual reality for Wade's social life. He considers Aech his best and only friend (cf. Cline 36 and Spielberg 00:05:35). Additionally, at least in the beginning, Wade knows his friend only in the virtual reality. He has no knowledge about her in the real world (cf. Cline 39). The fact that he does not know his only friend in real life highlights the superiority of the virtual reality. Cline writes about their relationship in detail and lets the reader know that although the two only know themselves online it is still a deep friendship based on trust and understanding. For instance, they respect each other's knowledge about the hunt in general. Although they are friends, they do not want to work together to find the Easter egg in the beginning. When Wade obtained the Copper key, he was very careful not to drop any hints while talking to Aech. Aech appreciated this, as she wanted to get to the key and the portal without support (cf. ibid. 123). Still, Parzival gives him a little hint at the end of the conversation, which again Aech appreciates and is thankful for (cf. ibid.). This shows that their friendship is based on a profound understanding of each other. Same is seen in the movie: their trust and their friendship are highlighted in the first scene in

Aech's chatroom (cf. Spielberg 00:40:30 - 00:41:57). They talk about Parzival's crush for Art3mis. The scene has an overall comfortable atmosphere with warm lightning and soft music which all lead to a friendly mood. Hence, this strengthens the aspect of their friendship being a fulfilled and happy one. Furthermore, their friendship originated in the virtual world and passes over to reality as well.

As the virtual reality created such a strong friendship, the characters have no problem of acting and feeling the same way in the real world. The reader and viewer get a hint of that when Wade's trailer and the stacks are destroyed by the IOI. Although this does not affect Wade's avatar Parzival Aech still lets him know that she cares: *"We will make them pay for this."* (Cline 149). Their friendship seems to be transcendent as Aech cares for both Wade and Parzival. Later in the storylines, Wade meets Aech in reality who turns out to be a "young woman" (ibid. 318), his first reaction is feeling betrayed (cf. ibid.). Nevertheless, the feeling quickly changes, and he is happy about meeting his friend (cf. ibid f.). In the movie Wade also does not care about Aech being a woman. These scenes imply that identity comes with personality rather than outer appearance or gender. Although Aech has a different biological sex than the avatar, it does not change their friendship. Their friendship shows that the OASIS can create and support strong friendships that are not influenced by hiccups like these. Furthermore, the relationship between Parzival and Art3mis strengthens this notion.

The origins and development of Parzival's and Art3mis relationship within the virtual reality is similar to the one with Aech. They do not know each other in real life, still a deep friendship and love develops between them. They start to chat and exchange emails in the OASIS. Then they met in a private chatroom where they "played vintage board games, watched movies, and listened to music" (ibid. 174) and they went on "dates" (ibid. 178). In the movie they go on research for the remaining quests together and share their thoughts and ideas about the quests. They also go on a date for dancing. Art3mis and Parzival fully get to know each other and grow fond of each other solely in virtual reality. However, when it comes to their real life encounters the novel and the movie differ.

The characters meet at a different time in the novel and in the movie, this leads to a shift of importance of the virtual reality. In the novel Parzival's and Art3mis' relationship is carefully choreographed with a climax in the end of the novel. The climax is outside the virtual reality when they meet each other in person in reality (cf. ibid. 370). The movie works differently. Wade meets his friends including Art3mis in the middle of the movie and concours IOI together with them in the real world and in the virtual world. The relationship is thus not as reliant on the virtual reality as it is in the novel, as the novel waits until the very end to bring Wade and

Samantha together in the real world. Furthermore, through this the novel gives the story a chance to create tension and desire for reality. For instance, Parzival tells Art3mis that he wants to meet her in real life (cf. ibid. 177). This is the first time in which the protagonist mentions that he desires to experience something in real life and thus establishes the notion of superiority of the real world. This is a hint for the ending of the novel: "It occurred to me then that for the first time in as long as I can remember, I had absolutely no desire to log back into the OASIS." (ibid. 372) Thus, this glimpse of desire to life in reality turns into the wish to turn off the OASIS as a whole. Therefore, one can say that although the virtual reality is described being of utter importance, reality still wins, as the most trueful experience happens in the real world. Even though the movie lacks this development its ending is still similar, as here Wade also says that he wants to live his life in the real world (cf. Spielberg 02:05:05 and 02:08:58). Overall, one can say that the relationship with Art3mis highlights the strength of virtual reality as well as the importance of experiences in the real world.

3.4.   Video Games

Video Games play an important role in both storylines. In what notions they appear and what effect they bring along will be discussed in the following chapter. Games are on all sites important in *Ready Player One*, inside the story and outside. Stark states that "Ready Player One is both a story about games and a game itself [...]." (Stark 152) This is since the novel itself has an Easter Egg and motivates the readers to take part in a hunt themselves as there is a URL hidden in the text (cf. ibid. 154). The movie does not have such an Easter Egg for its viewers. However, video games are of importance in both the novel and the movie's story. As previously mentioned, the OASIS was initially meant to be an online video game. Thus, the base of the whole virtual world is a video game and even now there are people who use the OASIS as a game and level up their avatars in fights and quests. But there are also people who do not care about their level "or bother with the gaming aspects of the simulation at all." (Cline 50) Therefore, there is no new version of the OASIS, it rather developed and increased its functions. Furthermore, Halliday created the Oasis due to his love for video games (cf. ibid. 4). Therefore, video games are both technically and emotionally the base of the whole virtual reality and thus of importance to the world in the novel as well as the movie. Furthermore, the main topic of the story, the hunt, is a game itself.

The whole narrative of the story is happening around the hunt for Halliday's Easter egg. The game is structured into different parts or levels which build on one another. The notion of levels is highlighted by the naming of the novel's chapters. Each level contains riddles which

11

lead to finding the ultimate price: the Easter egg. The thought of the hunt being a game is strengthened by the existence of a high-score list: "[...] there was a high-score list like those that used to appear in old coin-operated videogames." (ibid. 7). The comparison of the hunt and traditional video games is directly made here and again later "It was a game anyone could play [...]" (ibid.). Thus, the hunt can be seen as a video game itself and therefore strengthens the importance of such in *Ready Player One*'s society. The hunt in the movie is structured similarly, but simultaneously "entirely different" (Ue 6). Still, there are quests to solve and games to win. There does also exist a high-score list. The list is hanging in the sky with colourful letters. When Parzival's name appears on the list for the first time, there is heroic music and fireworks (cf. Spielberg 00:28:21) which strengthen the notion of winning a game or at least a level. Moreover, video games play an important role in Wade's life as well.

All relationships of Wade are more or less influenced by video games. In the beginning of the novel Cline mentions Wade's mother and that Wade considers the memory of playing video games in the OASIS with his mother as one of his "happiest childhood memories" (Cline 18). Although his mother is only mentioned briefly in the story, Cline includes this memory which enhances the importance of video games in the novel. Parzival also spends a lot of time playing video games in the OASIS with Aech in the novel and the movie: "We also played a lot of videogames, of course. Aech and I had wasted countless hours on two-player classics [...]." (ibid. 39) Both play all videogames within the virtual reality. Moreover, the passion and knowledge for the games brings them closer together. Furthermore, their sympathy for each other is based on their obsession with the hunt. They both appreciate each other's work regarding the hunt and through this came to like each other even more: "He'd been my closest friend ever since." (ibid. 39) Hence, video games strengthen their friendship. A similar connection of video games and friendship can be seen in the relationship with Art3mis. They got to know each other due to the hunt in the first place. Although the staging of the hunt and the quests for receiving the keys are different in the novel and in the movie, one can still see a similarity in the first meeting of Art3mis and Parzival. In both instances they meet while trying to get the first key. In addition, there are several scenes in both versions which highlight video games as a central aspect in their relationship. For instance, in the movie Art3mis appreciates Parzival's knowledge of the hunt when she tests his knowledge (Spielberg 00:18:27). Or Parzival giving Art3mis a tip for beating the Artificial Intelligence in *Joust* to obtain the first key. Comparable to this is the scene where Parzival saves Art3mis from King Kong in the movie. In both instances, the hunt and Wade's knowledge about the game brings them closer together. Furthermore, there are video games within the game.

Knowledge about old video games play an important role too as appear repeatedly throughout the story and are the key of solving the hunt. For example, not only is the first key hidden on the planet Ludus in the novel as previously mentioned, moreover it is hidden with a quest based upon the classic game Dungeons & Dragons (cf. Cline 77). Moreover, to obtain the Copper key one must beat an AI at another classic game called *Joust* (cf. ibid. 80). This idea of games within games is repeated throughout almost all quests and tasks of the hunt (i.e., cf. ibid. 108). Hence, the overall importance of video games is highlighted in the novel. The movie depicts this differently. For instance, to obtain the first key you must finish a car race. This task is not based on a traditional game as in the novel, one rather needs deeper knowledge of Halliday in general to find the solution to drive backwards under the road. Thus, video games are not put forward but the character Halliday. Another aspect emphasizes the difference of importance of video games in both versions of the story.

The extra life Parzival gets in form of a coin is received differently. Whereas in the novel Parzival gains this coin after finishing a perfect Pac Man game (cf. ibid. 224), in the movie a butler who later is revealed as Ogden Morrow gives him the coin as a reward for perfect knowledge of Halliday's life. Therefore, there is no video game involved in the movie. However, the Pac-Man game "serves significant rhetorical and narrative functions" (Ue 4) and according to Ue illustrates the importance of the "potential of the past to benefit our futures" (ibid.). Hence, Wade has the skills to win the game because he knows that Halliday used to like this very game. Through his understanding he ultimately obtains the extra life. Thus, there can be seen a similarity to the scene in the movie. Still, the movie offers a less complex portrayal of Wade's understanding and does not involve a video game in this scene. In addition, the last quest in the hunt is the same in both sources: the video game Adventure. The protagonist wins it by knowing the location of the easter egg in the game. Consequently, here we have a strengthening of the importance of video games in both stories. Overall, video games are prominent in both the novel and the movie and play an integral part in the storytelling.

3.5.   Escapism

In both storylines it becomes clear that the real world is in very bad condition which is why people use virtual reality as an escape from the problems in the real world. This chapter discusses the motif of escapism in the novel and in the movie. The OASIS stands repeatedly in contrast with the real world. For instance, the first description of the OASIS is followed by a description of the real world which is facing numerous catastrophes such as: "The ongoing energy crisis. Catastrophic climate change. Widespread famine poverty, and disease. Half a dozen wars." (Cline 1) And virtual reality is leaving Wade "[…] to explore an entirely new world, very different from the one I'd known up until then." (ibid. 15) A similar contrast is made right after the description of the great educational possibilities in the OASIS. The author describes that earth is in a very bad condition. Human beings have caused the earth to fail and are leading nature to their own deaths: "Maybe it isn't a good idea to tell a newly arrived human being that he's been born into a world of chaos, pain, and poverty just in time to watch everything fall into pieces." (ibid. 18) The movie picks up this notion as well. After showing the poor living conditions in the stacks and mentioning several other problems on earth Wade says: "These days, reality is a bummer, everyone is looking for a way to escape." (Ready Player One 00:02:56 - 00:02:59) The people in *Ready Player One* try to escape the real world: "Characters contrast their grim apocalyptic reality with escapism through worldwide gaming in the OASIS, a massively multiplayer VR world allowing players to travel into space, experience high fantasy, attend lavish parties, or simply socialize with friends." (Patra 1663) As Patra states, the OASIS can be seen as a safe haven with limitless possibilities.

The motif of escapism is also seen in the life of the protagonist. The description of Wade's real-world home, the trailer park, is poor. He lives in this trailer with his aunt and fifteen other people (cf. Cline 13), the place "reeked of cat piss and abject poverty." (ibid.) In the movie Wade's home and the trailer park are depicted the same (cf. Ready Player One 00:01:14 - 00:02:35). Still, Wade considers advantages of their trailer as it is less crowded, bigger, and higher up than other trailers in the stack (cf. Ue 2). But mostly he is thankful for having access to virtual reality: "And I had the OASIS. My life wasn't so bad." (Cline 19) Besides the home in the trailer, Wade also has a hideout: "The van was my refuge." (ibid. 25). Wade's hideout mainly consists of gear for the OASIS. One could say that the OASIS is then a hideout in a hideout. The hideout is visually portrayed the same in the movie (cf. Spielberg 00:02:40). The wish to escape reality becomes even clearer when looking at Wade's social life. He feels uncomfortable in the real world as he has difficulties with social interactions. In virtual reality this is different. Here, he can talk and interact confidently with others (cf. ibid. 30). Although the OASIS is a secure place for him, he himself blames it for his lack of social skills: "[…] a side effect of spending most of my childhood inside the OASIS." (ibid. 30). Still, transferring to the virtual reality school was an escape for Wade. There, he must face no bullies and other difficult circumstances. On Ludus he feels safe: "No one could even touch me. In here, I was safe." (ibid. 32) Furthermore, he can escape his physical appearance. Wade describes himself being overweight and visibly poor. In the OASIS he is free to choose his physical appearance. He only faces limitations with his clothing, as he is just as poor in the OASIS as in the real world, he cannot afford expensive clothing for his avatar. Additionally, Nordstrom argues: "In a sense, the OASIS is the inverse of Wade's ordinary experiences." (Nordstrom 244) and "the OASIS as an online 'escape hatch' from reality." (ibid.) Hence, Wade can banish every problem he faces in the real world. The virtual world offers him a contrary life. Patra also uses the term "escape hatch" (Patra 1663) to describe video games as a way to escape reality. Wade uses games as well as the OASIS as an escape, since he fully invests himself to the hunt and shuts out the real world, as will be discussed later in this chapter in more detail. However, there is no real mentioning of such difficulties at school or social interactions and a thus resulting wish to escape in the movie. Moreover, the whole notion of escapism is depicted differently.

The novel and the movie portray Wade's attitude to the real world and the virtual world differently, or at least less dramatic. In both versions Wade is asked what he will do when he wins the hunt. In the novel he says that he wants to escape earth with a rocket and fly to the universe (cf. Cline 98). Whereas in the movie, he answers: "I've got tons of plans in the real world. I'd move into a huge mansion, buy a bunch of cool shit, not be poor." (Spielberg 00:19:05) These are two completely different things. In the movie Wade wants to engage with the real world, he does not want to turn his back on reality like he does in the novel. This difference is further strengthened as the stories continue. In the novel Wade moves into a small apartment and barricades himself inside. He vows: "Then I made a silent vow not to go outside again until I had completed my quest. I would abandon the real word altogether until I found the egg." (Cline 166) Here, he basically abandons earth altogether, as he wants to leave earth after he found the egg. During the time in the apartment Wade sees all tasks outside the OASIS as a burden:

> The narrator feels that the hour after his waking up and cleaning and exercising his physical body is his most tedious part of life and for him now the life inside OASIS is the real life and the previous life which he used to lead entirely on physical plane of reality now seems to be a wasted land meaningless life. (Patra 1666)

As Patra states, Wade entirely trades his life in the real world for a life in the OASIS. Additionally, he later imprisons himself willingly in the IOI prison to save the OASIS. He thus risks his own life and well being in the real world to save his virtual reality. The movie does neither include the apartment nor does Wade imprison himself in the IOI quarters. Here, Art3mis is the one risking her life. Overall, escapism is more prominent in the novel. The movie barely touches upon the motif without going into a more detailed portrayal or discourse.

4. Conclusion

Overall, this paper has shown that the initial statement that the novel offers a more profound and deeper representation of the OASIS is true. Although the movie and the novel share similarities, the novel manages to create a more thoughtful virtual reality. This has also an effect on the novel's characters and their development. Here, the movie lacks important scenes and has shifted its focus away from the importance of the virtual world in the society. It almost seems as if it was too easy to leave the OASIS in the end compared to the novel which offers a carefully choreographed story that leads to the character's peace with reality.

The overall technology of the OASIS is the same in both the novel and the movie. Furthermore, theoretically speaking one can say that the technology used for the OASIS is possible in our reality and is partly in use already. Still, especially the novel offers views on numerous possibilities that could be adapted in our reality as well. Foremost there is the aspect of education. Scholars already ask for an integration of virtual reality in education, the novel strengthens this thought by showing that virtual schools could make education accessible for everyone and introduce new teaching methods that could enhance motivation in both students and teachers.

The representation of friendship is similar in both versions as well, at least in the beginning. In both instances Wade meets his friends in the virtual world. The OASIS offers ways of communications that are the same as in the real world, including gestures and facial expressions. A big difference is made in movie since here the characters meet much sooner in the real world. This results in putting the virtual reality more in the background, thus it loses importance. Furthermore, the first meeting of Samantha and Wade has a much greater effect in the novel as Cline waits until the very end to make them meet in person. The novel also creates a stronger feeling of 'finding a way back to reality'.

When it comes to video games both versions of the story stress their importance for the story in general, but also for the development of the character's relationship. Video games are omnipresent due to the hunt and due to the overall video game nostalgia in the story. However, again the novel creates a deeper view into the topic and illustrates the theme in more detail. Instances like the quest of the first key and the perfect Pac Man game are the main differences with the biggest effect. They offer the novel a more profound representation of the importance of video games. Moreover, the notion of escapism is much more present in the novel as well. The movie only hints on this thought but generally seems to omit this theme. The biggest proof of this is the fact that the movie changed the scene in which Wade talks about his plan after finding the Easter egg. Whereas the novel clearly states that Wade wants to escape the earth and thus reality, the movie just puts a stereotypical answer into the scene. Here, the movie misses a great chance for character development and profundity.

Summing up, the novel offers much more variety and profundity. It generally illustrates more ideas in the virtual reality and even comes along with aspects we could make use of in our reality. The movie on the other hand shows similar technological standards but misses this profundity. Still, there are more aspects to analyse in the stories. For instance, can the OASIS really be considered a virtual reality or would another definition like Extended Reality fit better as it is not purely a simulation since it interacts and intervenes highly with the real world.

Bibliography

Primary Literature

Cline, Ernest. *Ready Player One*. Broadway Books, 2011.

Spielberg, Steven, director. *Ready Player One*. Warner Bros, 2018.

Secondary Literature

Chaturvedi, Alok R., et al. "Design Principles for Virtual Worlds." *MIS Quarterly*, vol. 35, no. 3, 2011, pp. 673-684.

Crawford, Matthew B. "Virtual Reality as Moral Ideal." *The New Atlantis,* no. 44, 2015, pp.28-36.

Dörner, Ralf, et al. "Einleitung." *Virtual und Augmented Reality (VR/AR)*, edited by Ralf Dörner, et al. Springer, 2013, pp. 241-294.

Downey, Steve. "History of the (Virtual) World." *The Journal of Technology Studies*, vol 40, no 1/2, 2014, pp. 54-66.

Fairfield, Joshua A. T. "Mixed Reality: How the Laws of Virtual Worlds Govern Everyday Life." *Berkeley Technology Law Journal*, vol. 27, no.1, 2012, pp. 55-116.

Fink, Charlie. "The Reality of Virtual Reality In 'Ready Player One'." *Forbes*, 23 Oct. 2017, https://www.forbes.com/sites/charliefink/2017/10/23/the-reality-of-virtual-reality-in-ready-player-one/?sh=5006623f20d0 . Accessed August 15th, 2021.

Johnson, Laurence F., and Alan H. Levine. "Virtual Worlds: Inherently Immersive, Highly Social Learning Spaces." *Theory Into Practice*, vol. 47, no. 2, 2008, pp. 161-170.

Langer, Elle. *Medieninnovationen AR und VR*. Springer Vieweg, 2020.

Lasko-Harvill, Ann. "Identity and Mask in Virtual Reality." *Discourse*, vol. 14, no. 2, 1992, pp. 222-234.

Nasyrov, Rinat R., and Peter S. Excell. "Creation of Interactive Virtual Reality Scenarios as a Training and Education Tool." *Technology, Design and the Arts – Opportunities and Challenges*, edited by Rae Earnshaw, et al., Springer Open, 2020, pp. 353-371.

Nordstrom, Justin. ""A Pleasant Place for the World to Hide": Exploring Themes of Utopian Play in Ready Player One." *Interdisciplinary Literary Studies*, vol. 18, no. 2, 2016, pp. 238-256.

Patra, Indrajit. "To Immerse is to Escape: Analyzing the Power of Simulacra and Simulation in Ernest Cline's Ready Player One and Ready Player Two." *Ilkogretim Online – Elementary Education Online*, vol. 20, no. 1, 2021, pp. 1658-1671.

Psotka, Joseph. "Educational Games and Virtual Reality as Disruptive Technologies." *Journal of Educational Technology & Society*, vol. 16, no. 2, 2013, pp. 69-80.

Saunders, Carol, et al. "Virtual Space and Place: Theory And Test." *MIS Quarterly*, vol. 35, no. 4, 2011, pp. 1079-1098.

Stark, Doug. "Ludic Literature: *Ready Player One* as Didactive Fiction for the Neoliberal Subject." *Playing the Field: Video Games and American Studies,* edited by Sascha Pöhlmann, DeGruyter, 2019, pp. 151-172.

Stevens, Jane Ellen. "The Growing Reality of Virtual Reality." *BioScience*, vol. 45, no. 7, 1995, pp. 435-439.

Ue, Tom, and James Munday. "Past, Present, and Place: Setting in Cline's *Ready Player One*." *The Palgrave Encyclopedia of Urban Literary Studies*, edited by Tambling J., Palgrave Macmillan, Cham, 2021.